INTRODUCTION

Christmas with the Saucy Pig Family:

The Ultimate BBQ Recipes for the Holiday Season

Welcome to Christmas with The Saucy Pig Family!

Join us as we unveil the secrets behind our cherished Christmas celebrations. We've often been asked about our festive traditions, the flavors that adorn our table, and the joyous atmosphere we cultivate. For us, Christmas is more than a day; it's a heartfelt invitation to gather around the table with family, friends, and even newfound companions who leave as cherished friends.

In the spirit of togetherness, our table always sets a place for absent friends, honoring their memory and spirit amidst our festivities. Christmas is a time for warmth, laughter, and creating lasting memories. We believe in opening our doors to share not just our favorite dishes but the love and laughter that make this season truly special.

In this collection, we invite you to embark on a culinary adventure with us. Explore our treasured recipes, crafted with care and tradition, to make your Christmas and every meal a celebration. Here's to good food, delightful drinks, and the joy of great company. May your festive season be filled with delectable flavors and your New Year brim with culinary delights!

Cheers to the heartwarming and delicious festivities ahead!

The Saucy Pig Family

MEET THE TEAM

Meet the dynamic duo behind the sizzling sensation—the Saucy Pig Team!

Chunkz and George, affectionately known as The Saucy Pig and The Saucy Piglet, aren't just a father and son; they're a culinary force. Chunkz, the seasoned chef with a flair for flavors, mentors his eager apprentice, George, in the art of crafting delectable dishes that tantalize taste buds. Their passion for all things savory and their infectious enthusiasm are the secret ingredients that make their cooking adventures a feast for the senses. Whether they're experimenting with new recipes or delighting fans with their tried-and-true classics, the Saucy Pig Team brings creativity, warmth, and a whole lot of sauciness to the kitchen.

What's On The Menu

Starters:

1. Bacon-Wrapped Jalapeño Poppers
2. Salmon Crostini with Cream Cheese
3. Deviled Eggs
4. Mozzarella and Tomato Skewers
5. Brisket Chili
6. BBQ Stuffed Mushrooms
7. Shrimp Cocktail
8. Cheese and Charcuterie Board
9. Buffalo Cauliflower Bites (Vegetarian)
10. Artichoke Dip (Vegetarian)

Main Course:

1. Smoked Turkey with Herb Butter
2. Smoked Prime Rib
3. Smoked Ham with Pineapple Glaze
4. Smoked Whole Chicken with BBQ Rub
5. Smoked Beef Ribs
6. Smoked Pork Shoulder with BBQ Sauce
7. Smoked Rack of Lamb with Mint Jelly
8. Smoked Tofurky (Vegetarian)
9. Smoked Portobello Mushrooms with Balsamic Glaze (Vegetarian)
10. Smoked Stuffed Bell Peppers (Vegetarian)

Side Dishes:

1. Smoked Mac and Cheese
2. Smoked Brussels Sprouts with Bacon
3. Smoked Corn on the Cob with Garlic Butter
4. Smoked Potato Salad
5. Smoked Baked Beans
6. Smoked Asparagus with Lemon and Parmesan
7. Smoked Collard Greens
8. Smoked Sweet Potato Casserole

9. Smoked Cabbage Steaks
10. Smoked Veggie Skewers (Vegetarian)

Desserts:

1. Smoked Peach Cobbler
2. Smoked Chocolate Pecan Pie
3. Smoked Banana Splits
4. Smoked Apple Crisp
5. Smoked Cherry Cheesecake
6. Smoked Pineapple Upside-Down Cake
7. Smoked Pumpkin Pie
8. Smoked Mixed Berry Galette
9. Smoked Bread Pudding
10. Smoked Chocolate Fondue (Vegetarian)

Sauces and Condiments:

1. Homemade BBQ Sauce
2. Smoked Aioli
3. Smoked Chipotle Ketchup
4. Smoked Garlic Butter
5. Smoked Jalapeño Hot Sauce
6. Smoked Pickles
7. Smoked Salsa
8. Smoked Mustard Sauce
9. Smoked Cranberry Sauce
10. Smoked Honey Glaze

Beverages:

1. Smoked Old Fashioned Cocktail
2. Smoked Apple Cider
3. Smoked Lemonade
4. Smoked Iced Tea
5. Smoked Moscow Mule
6. Smoked Cranberry Punch
7. Smoked Hot Chocolate

8. Smoked Coffee
9. Smoked Eggnog
10. Smoked Sangria

Let the festivities begin...

STARTERS

Bacon-Wrapped Jalapeño Poppers

Ingredients:

12 fresh jalapeño peppers (about 225 grams)
8 ounces (225 grams) cream cheese, softened
1 cup (115 grams) shredded cheddar cheese
1 teaspoon (5 grams) garlic powder
12 slices bacon

Instructions:

Preparing the Jalapeño Poppers:

1. Cut the jalapeño peppers in half lengthwise and remove the seeds and membranes. Use caution and gloves to avoid getting the jalapeño oils on your skin.

2. In a mixing bowl, combine the softened cream cheese, shredded cheddar cheese, and garlic powder. Mix until well combined.

3. Fill each jalapeño half with the cheese mixture.

4. Wrap each stuffed jalapeño with a slice of bacon and secure with toothpicks.

Smoking Process:

1. Preheat your BBQ smoker to 250°F (120°C).

2. Place the bacon-wrapped jalapeño poppers on the smoker grates.

3. Smoke the poppers for approximately 1 to 1.5 hours or until the bacon is crispy and the jalapeños are tender.

Resting:

- Remove the poppers from the smoker and let them rest for about 5 minutes before serving.

Storage Recommendations:

- If you have leftovers, store them in an airtight container in the refrigerator.

- Reheat in an oven or on the smoker for best results.

- Consume leftover poppers within 2-3 days for optimal freshness.

Salmon Crostini with Cream Cheese

Ingredients:

1 baguette (about 300 grams)
8 ounces (225 grams) smoked salmon
8 ounces (225 grams) cream cheese, softened
1/4 cup (60 ml) sour cream
1 tablespoon (15 ml) fresh lemon juice
2 tablespoons (30 grams) capers, drained and chopped
2 tablespoons (30 grams) fresh dill, chopped
Salt and black pepper to taste

Instructions:

Preparing the Crostini:

1. Preheat your BBQ smoker to 250°F (120°C).

2. Slice the baguette into 1/2-inch (1.25 cm) thick diagonal slices.

3. Place the baguette slices on the smoker grates and smoke for about 15-20 minutes or until they have a subtle smoky flavor and a slightly crispy texture. Remove and set aside.

Cream Cheese Spread:

1. In a mixing bowl, combine the softened cream cheese, sour cream, fresh lemon juice, chopped capers, and fresh dill. Mix until the ingredients are well incorporated.

2. Season the cream cheese spread with salt and black pepper to taste. Adjust the seasoning according to your preference.

Assembling the Crostini:

1. Take each smoked baguette slice and spread a generous amount of the cream cheese mixture onto one side.

2. Place a small piece of smoked salmon on top of the cream cheese spread on each baguette slice.

3. Garnish with additional fresh dill or capers if desired.

Resting:

- Allow the assembled crostini to rest for about 5 minutes to let the flavors meld together.

Storage Recommendations:

- If you have leftovers, store them in an airtight container in the refrigerator.

- Consume leftover crostini within 2-3 days for optimal freshness. Note that the texture of the smoked baguette may change slightly upon refrigeration.

Deviled Eggs

Ingredients:

6 large eggs
2 tablespoons (30 grams) mayonnaise
1 teaspoon (5 grams) Dijon mustard
1 teaspoon (5 grams) white vinegar
1/2 teaspoon (2.5 grams) granulated sugar
1/8 teaspoon (0.6 grams) salt
1/8 teaspoon (0.6 grams) black pepper
1/4 teaspoon (1.25 grams) paprika, for garnish
Fresh chives or parsley, for garnish (optional)

Instructions:

Smoking Process:

1. Preheat your BBQ smoker to 250°F (120°C).

2. Place the eggs directly on the smoker grates. Smoke the eggs for about 30-40 minutes to infuse them with a subtle smoky flavor.

3. After smoking, remove the eggs from the smoker and let them cool to room temperature.

Preparing the Deviled Eggs:

1. Once the smoked eggs have cooled, peel them carefully.
2. Cut each egg in half lengthwise, and gently scoop out the yolks into a mixing bowl. Place the egg whites on a serving platter.
3. Mash the egg yolks with a fork until they are crumbled.
4. To the mashed yolks, add mayonnaise, Dijon mustard, white vinegar, granulated sugar, salt, and black pepper. Mix until you have a smooth, creamy filling.
5. Spoon or pipe the egg yolk mixture back into the egg white halves.
6. Sprinkle each deviled egg with a pinch of paprika for garnish. You can also add fresh chives or parsley if desired.

Resting:

- Allow the deviled eggs to rest in the refrigerator for at least 30 minutes before serving. This allows the flavors to meld together.

Storage Recommendations:

- If you have leftovers, store them in an airtight container in the refrigerator.
- Consume leftover deviled eggs within 2-3 days for optimal freshness.

Mozzarella and Tomato Skewers

Ingredients:

12 cherry tomatoes
12 small fresh mozzarella balls (about 225 grams)
12 fresh basil leaves
Olive oil, for drizzling
Balsamic glaze, for drizzling
Salt and black pepper, to taste
Wooden skewers, soaked in water for 30 minutes

Instructions:

Smoking Process:

1. Preheat your BBQ smoker to 250°F (120°C).

2. While the smoker is heating up, assemble the skewers. Thread a cherry tomato, a fresh mozzarella ball, and a fresh basil leaf onto each wooden skewer. Repeat until you have 12 skewers.

3. Drizzle the assembled skewers with olive oil and season with salt and black pepper to taste.

4. Place the skewers on the smoker grates.

5. Smoke the skewers for about 20-25 minutes or until the tomatoes are softened and the mozzarella begins to develop a subtle smoky flavor.

Resting:

- Remove the mozzarella and tomato skewers from the smoker and let them rest for a few minutes before serving.

- Just before serving, drizzle balsamic glaze over the skewers for an extra burst of flavor.

Storage Recommendations:

- If you have leftovers, store them in an airtight container in the refrigerator.

- Consume leftover mozzarella and tomato skewers within 2-3 days for optimal freshness. The texture of the mozzarella may change slightly upon refrigeration, but the flavor will still be delicious.

Brisket Chili

Ingredients:

1.5 pounds (680 grams) smoked beef brisket, diced
1 medium onion, chopped
3 cloves garlic, minced
1 red bell pepper, chopped
1 green bell pepper, chopped
2 (14-ounce/400 grams) cans diced tomatoes
1 (14-ounce/400 grams) can kidney beans, drained and rinsed
1 (14-ounce/400 grams) can black beans, drained and rinsed
2 cups (480 ml) beef broth
2 tablespoons (30 grams) chili powder
1 tablespoon (15 grams) ground cumin
1 teaspoon (5 grams) paprika
1/2 teaspoon (2.5 grams) cayenne pepper (adjust to taste)
Salt and black pepper, to taste
Olive oil, for cooking

Instructions:

BBQ Smoking Process:

1. Preheat your BBQ smoker to 250°F (120°C).

2. Place the smoked beef brisket on the smoker grates. Smoke the brisket for about 2-3 hours to enhance its smoky flavor. Remove it from the smoker and dice it into small pieces.

Preparing the Chili:

1. In a large pot or Dutch oven, heat a drizzle of olive oil over medium heat.

2. Add the chopped onion and cook for about 2-3 minutes until it becomes translucent.

3. Stir in the minced garlic and cook for another 30 seconds until fragrant.

4. Add the red and green bell peppers and cook for about 3-4 minutes until they start to soften.

5. Add the diced smoked brisket to the pot and cook for an additional 2-3 minutes, allowing it to mix with the other ingredients.

6. Pour in the diced tomatoes, kidney beans, black beans, and beef broth.

7. Stir in the chili powder, ground cumin, paprika, cayenne pepper, salt, and black pepper.

8. Bring the mixture to a boil, then reduce the heat to low, cover, and simmer for about 1.5 to 2 hours, stirring occasionally. The flavors will meld together, and the chili will thicken.

Resting:

- Remove the pot from heat and let the chili rest for about 10-15 minutes before serving. This allows the flavors to further develop.

Storage Recommendations:

- If you have leftovers, store them in an airtight container in the refrigerator.

- Reheat the brisket chili in a pot on the stove or in the microwave for a quick meal.

- Consume leftover chili within 3-4 days for optimal freshness. The flavors tend to deepen over time, making it even more delicious.

Stuffed Mushrooms

Ingredients:

12 large white mushrooms (about 450 grams)
1/2 cup (115 grams) cream cheese, softened
1/4 cup (30 grams) shredded cheddar cheese
1/4 cup (30 grams) grated Parmesan cheese
2 cloves garlic, minced
2 tablespoons (30 grams) fresh parsley, chopped
1/4 teaspoon (1.25 grams) black pepper
1/4 teaspoon (1.25 grams) paprika
1/4 teaspoon (1.25 grams) cayenne pepper (adjust to taste)
Salt, to taste
Olive oil, for brushing

Instructions:

BBQ Smoking Process:

1. Preheat your BBQ smoker to 250°F (120°C).

2. Clean the mushrooms and remove the stems. You can use a spoon to gently scoop out the gills to create more space for the filling.

3. In a mixing bowl, combine the softened cream cheese, shredded cheddar cheese, grated Parmesan cheese, minced garlic, chopped fresh parsley, black pepper, paprika, and cayenne pepper. Mix until all the ingredients are well incorporated. Season with salt to taste.

4. Stuff each mushroom cap with the cream cheese mixture, filling them generously.

5. Lightly brush the outside of the stuffed mushrooms with olive oil to prevent sticking and to enhance the texture when smoked.

6. Place the stuffed mushrooms on the smoker grates.

7. Smoke the mushrooms for about 45 minutes to 1 hour, or until they are tender and have absorbed a subtle smoky flavor.

Resting:

- Remove the stuffed mushrooms from the smoker and let them rest for about 5 minutes before serving.

Storage Recommendations:

- If you have leftovers, store them in an airtight container in the refrigerator.
- Reheat the stuffed mushrooms in an oven or on the smoker for the best results.
- Consume leftover stuffed mushrooms within 2-3 days for optimal freshness. The smoky flavors may intensify over time, making them even more delicious.

Smoked Shrimp Cocktail

Ingredients:

1 pound (450 grams) large shrimp, peeled and deveined
1 tablespoon (15 ml) olive oil
1 teaspoon (5 grams) paprika
1/2 teaspoon (2.5 grams) garlic powder
1/4 teaspoon (1.25 grams) cayenne pepper (adjust to taste)
Salt and black pepper, to taste
1/4 cup (60 ml) cocktail sauce
1 lemon, cut into wedges
Fresh parsley, for garnish (optional)

Instructions:

Smoking Process:

1. Preheat your BBQ smoker to 250°F (120°C).

2. In a mixing bowl, combine the peeled and deveined shrimp with olive oil, paprika, garlic powder, cayenne pepper, salt, and black pepper. Toss to coat the shrimp evenly.

3. Thread the seasoned shrimp onto skewers or use a grill basket to keep them from falling through the smoker grates.

4. Place the shrimp skewers or grill basket on the smoker grates.

5. Smoke the shrimp for approximately 15-20 minutes or until they turn pink and are cooked through. They will also absorb a subtle smoky flavor during this time.

Resting:

- Remove the smoked shrimp from the smoker and let them rest for about 5 minutes.

Assembling the Shrimp Cocktail:

- Arrange the smoked shrimp on a serving platter.

- Serve with cocktail sauce and lemon wedges for dipping.

- Garnish with fresh parsley if desired.

Storage Recommendations:

- If you have leftovers, store them in an airtight container in the refrigerator.

- Serve the leftover smoked shrimp cold as a snack or in salads within 2-3 days for optimal freshness.

Cheese and Charcuterie Board

Ingredients:

4-6 types of your favorite cheeses (e.g., cheddar, brie, gouda, blue cheese, camembert)
4-6 types of cured meats (e.g., prosciutto, salami, chorizo, smoked ham)
1 cup (150 grams) mixed olives
1/2 cup (75 grams) mixed nuts (e.g., almonds, cashews)
1/2 cup (75 grams) dried fruits (e.g., apricots, figs)
1/2 cup (75 grams) fresh fruits (e.g., grapes, apple slices)
1/4 cup (30 grams) pickles or gherkins
1/4 cup (30 grams) whole grain mustard
1/4 cup (30 grams) honey
Assorted crackers and bread
Fresh herbs and edible flowers for garnish (optional)

Smoking Process:

1. Preheat your BBQ smoker to 250°F (120°C).

2. While the smoker is heating up, prepare a foil pouch with wood chips (e.g., hickory, applewood) to create smoke. Place the foil pouch directly on the smoker's coals or heat source.

3. Arrange the cheese and charcuterie items on a large serving board or platter, leaving space for the smoked items.

4. Place the mixed olives, mixed nuts, dried fruits, fresh fruits, and pickles on the board.

5. Once the smoker is ready and producing smoke, place some of the cheeses and cured meats on the smoker grates. Smoke them for about 15-20 minutes, or until they develop a subtle smoky flavor.

6. Remove the smoked items from the smoker and place them on the board alongside the non-smoked items.

Resting:

- Allow the smoked cheeses and charcuterie to rest for a few minutes before serving to let the flavors meld.

Serving:

- Serve the cheese and charcuterie board with whole grain mustard and honey for dipping, along with assorted crackers and bread.
- Garnish with fresh herbs and edible flowers if desired.

Storage Recommendations:

- If you have leftovers, store the smoked and non-smoked items separately in airtight containers in the refrigerator.
- Consume leftover items within 2-3 days for optimal freshness. Smoked items may lose some of their smoky flavor over time but will still be delicious.

Buffalo Cauliflower Bites (Vegetarian)

Ingredients:

1 medium cauliflower head (about 2.2 pounds or 1 kg), cut into bite-sized florets
1/2 cup (60 grams) all-purpose flour
1/2 cup (120 ml) milk (dairy or plant-based)
1 teaspoon (5 grams) garlic powder
1 teaspoon (5 grams) onion powder
1/2 teaspoon (2.5 grams) paprika
1/4 teaspoon (1.25 grams) cayenne pepper (adjust to taste)
Salt and black pepper, to taste
1/4 cup (60 grams) unsalted butter, melted
1/2 cup (120 ml) hot sauce (adjust to taste)
Cooking spray or oil for greasing

BBQ Smoking Process:

1. Preheat your BBQ smoker to 250°F (120°C) using indirect heat.

2. In a mixing bowl, whisk together the flour, milk, garlic powder, onion powder, paprika, cayenne pepper, salt, and black pepper until you have a smooth batter.

3. Dip each cauliflower floret into the batter, ensuring it's well coated, and then place it on a greased or lined baking sheet.

4. Transfer the battered cauliflower florets to the BBQ smoker grates.

5. Smoke the cauliflower for about 45 minutes to 1 hour, or until they are tender and have a smoky flavor. You can occasionally baste them with some melted butter during the smoking process for added flavor.

Resting:

- Remove the smoked cauliflower bites from the smoker and let them rest for about 5 minutes.

- While the cauliflower is resting, mix the melted butter and hot sauce in a separate bowl to create the Buffalo sauce.

Coating with Buffalo Sauce:

- Toss the smoked cauliflower bites in the Buffalo sauce until they are evenly coated.

Serving:

- Serve the Buffalo cauliflower bites with celery sticks and your choice of dipping sauce (e.g., ranch or blue cheese).

Storage Recommendations:

- If you have leftovers, store them in an airtight container in the refrigerator.

- Reheat the Buffalo cauliflower bites in an oven or on the smoker for best results.

- Consume leftover cauliflower bites within 2-3 days for optimal freshness. The smoky flavor may intensify over time, making them even more delicious.

Artichoke Dip (Vegetarian)

Ingredients:

1 (14-ounce/400 grams) can of artichoke hearts, drained and chopped
1 (10-ounce/285 grams) package of frozen spinach, thawed and drained
1 cup (240 ml) mayonnaise
1 cup (240 ml) sour cream
1 cup (90 grams) grated Parmesan cheese
1 cup (90 grams) shredded mozzarella cheese
3 cloves garlic, minced
1/2 teaspoon (2.5 grams) salt
1/4 teaspoon (1.25 grams) black pepper
1/4 teaspoon (1.25 grams) red pepper flakes (adjust to taste)
Olive oil, for greasing

BBQ Smoking Process:

1. Preheat your BBQ smoker to 250°F (120°C) using indirect heat.

2. In a large mixing bowl, combine the chopped artichoke hearts, thawed and drained spinach, mayonnaise, sour cream, grated Parmesan cheese, shredded

mozzarella cheese, minced garlic, salt, black pepper, and red pepper flakes. Mix until all ingredients are well incorporated.

3. Transfer the mixture to an oven-safe dish suitable for smoking.

4. Place the dish with the artichoke dip on the smoker grates.

5. Smoke the dip for approximately 30-40 minutes, or until it is heated through and has absorbed a subtle smoky flavor. You can occasionally stir the dip for even smoking.

Resting:

- Remove the smoked artichoke dip from the smoker and let it rest for about 5 minutes before serving.

Serving:

- Serve the artichoke dip with tortilla chips, crackers, or sliced baguette for dipping.

Storage Recommendations:

- If you have leftovers, store them in an airtight container in the refrigerator.

- Reheat the artichoke dip in an oven or on the smoker for best results.

- Consume leftover dip within 2-3 days for optimal freshness. The smoky flavor may intensify over time, enhancing its deliciousness.

MAIN COURSE

Smoked Turkey with Herb Butter

Ingredients:

1 whole turkey (12-14 pounds / 5.4-6.4 kg)
1 cup (230 grams) unsalted butter, softened
2 tablespoons (30 grams) fresh rosemary, finely chopped
2 tablespoons (30 grams) fresh thyme, finely chopped
2 tablespoons (30 grams) fresh sage, finely chopped
4 cloves garlic, minced
Zest of 1 lemon
Salt and black pepper, to taste
Olive oil, for brushing

Smoking Process:

1. Preheat your BBQ smoker to 275°F (135°C) using indirect heat.

2. Rinse the turkey thoroughly under cold water and pat it dry with paper towels.

3. In a mixing bowl, combine the softened unsalted butter, chopped fresh rosemary, thyme, sage, minced garlic, lemon zest, salt, and black pepper. Mix until all ingredients are well incorporated.

4. Carefully separate the skin from the turkey breast by gently sliding your hand under the skin, being careful not to tear it.

5. Spread the herb butter mixture under the skin of the turkey, covering as much of the breast meat as possible. Massage the skin to distribute the herb butter evenly.

6. Brush the outside of the turkey with olive oil to help the skin crisp and brown nicely during smoking.

7. Place the turkey on the smoker grates, breast-side up.

8. Smoke the turkey at 275°F (135°C) for approximately 30-40 minutes per pound (0.45 kg) of turkey, or until the internal temperature of the thickest part of the breast and thigh reaches 165°F (74°C) on a meat thermometer.

9. Once done, carefully remove the turkey from the smoker and transfer it to a cutting board.

Resting:

- Allow the smoked turkey to rest, loosely tented with foil, for about 20-30 minutes before carving. This allows the juices to redistribute and results in juicier meat.

Storage Recommendations:

- If you have leftovers, store the carved turkey in airtight containers or sealed bags in the refrigerator.

- Consume leftover turkey within 3-4 days for optimal freshness. You can also freeze leftover turkey for longer storage. Reheat gently in the oven or microwave before serving.

Smoked Prime Rib

Ingredients:

1 bone-in prime rib roast (about 8-10 pounds / 3.6-4.5 kg)
4 tablespoons (60 grams) kosher salt
2 tablespoons (30 grams) black pepper
2 tablespoons (30 grams) garlic powder
2 tablespoons (30 grams) onion powder
2 tablespoons (30 grams) paprika
2 tablespoons (30 grams) dried thyme
2 tablespoons (30 grams) dried rosemary
2 tablespoons (30 grams) dried oregano
Olive oil, for brushing

Smoking Process:

1. Preheat your BBQ smoker to 225°F (107°C) using indirect heat.

2. In a bowl, combine the kosher salt, black pepper, garlic powder, onion powder, paprika, dried thyme, dried rosemary, and dried oregano to create a dry rub.

3. Pat the prime rib roast dry with paper towels and brush it lightly with olive oil.

4. Generously rub the dry seasoning mixture all over the prime rib, ensuring it's evenly coated.

5. Place the prime rib roast on the smoker grates, fat-side up.

6. Smoke the prime rib at 225°F (107°C) until it reaches your desired internal temperature. For medium-rare, aim for an internal temperature of around 130-135°F (54-57°C) measured with a meat thermometer inserted into the thickest part of the roast, away from the bone.

7. The smoking time will vary depending on the size of the roast and your desired doneness. Estimate approximately 30-35 minutes per pound (0.45 kg) of meat.

8. Once the prime rib reaches the desired internal temperature, remove it from the smoker and transfer it to a cutting board.

Resting:

- Tent the smoked prime rib loosely with foil and let it rest for about 20-30 minutes before carving. This resting period allows the juices to redistribute throughout the meat, resulting in juicier slices.

Storage Recommendations:

- If you have leftovers, wrap the carved prime rib tightly in foil or store it in an airtight container in the refrigerator.

- Consume leftover prime rib within 3-4 days for optimal freshness. Reheat gently in the oven to retain its tenderness before serving again.

Smoked Ham with Pineapple Glaze

Ingredients:

1 fully cooked bone-in ham, about 8-10 pounds (3.6-4.5 kg)
1 cup (240 ml) pineapple juice
1/2 cup (120 ml) honey
1/4 cup (60 ml) orange juice
1/4 cup (60 ml) brown sugar
2 tablespoons (30 ml) Dijon mustard
1 teaspoon (5 ml) ground cinnamon
1/2 teaspoon (2.5 ml) ground cloves
1/4 teaspoon (1.25 ml) ground nutmeg
Whole cloves (optional for decoration)

Smoking Process:

1. Preheat your BBQ smoker to 250°F (120°C) using indirect heat.

2. Place the fully cooked ham on the smoker grates and cover it with foil.

3. Smoke the ham at 250°F (120°C) for approximately 2-3 hours, or until the internal temperature reaches about 140-145°F (60-63°C) when measured with a meat thermometer.

4. While the ham is smoking, prepare the pineapple glaze.

Pineapple Glaze:

1. In a saucepan over medium heat, combine the pineapple juice, honey, orange juice, brown sugar, Dijon mustard, ground cinnamon, ground cloves, and ground nutmeg.

2. Bring the mixture to a gentle simmer, stirring occasionally. Let it simmer for about 15-20 minutes until it thickens slightly and reduces by about one-third.

3. Remove the glaze from heat and set it aside.

Finishing the Ham:

1. Once the ham reaches the desired internal temperature, remove it from the smoker and increase the smoker's temperature to 325°F (163°C).

2. Brush the smoked ham generously with the prepared pineapple glaze. If desired, insert whole cloves into the ham for decoration.

3. Return the glazed ham to the smoker and cook for an additional 30-45 minutes at 325°F (163°C) to set the glaze and caramelize it slightly.

Resting:

- Remove the smoked ham from the smoker and let it rest, loosely covered with foil, for about 15-20 minutes before carving.

Storage Recommendations:

- If you have leftovers, store the sliced ham in an airtight container or wrap it tightly in foil in the refrigerator.

- Consume leftover ham within 3-4 days for optimal freshness. Reheat gently in the oven or microwave before serving again.

Smoked Whole Chicken with BBQ Rub

Ingredients:

1 whole chicken (approximately 4-5 pounds / 1.8-2.3 kg)
4 tablespoons (60 grams) brown sugar
2 tablespoons (30 grams) smoked paprika
1 tablespoon (15 grams) garlic powder
1 tablespoon (15 grams) onion powder
1 tablespoon (15 grams) salt
1 tablespoon (15 grams) black pepper
1 teaspoon (5 grams) cayenne pepper
2 tablespoons (30 ml) olive oil

Smoking Process:

1. Preheat your BBQ smoker to 225°F (107°C) using indirect heat.

2. Rinse the whole chicken under cold water and pat it dry with paper towels.

3. In a bowl, combine the brown sugar, smoked paprika, garlic powder, onion powder, salt, black pepper, and cayenne pepper to create the dry rub.

4. Drizzle the olive oil over the chicken and massage it evenly onto the surface.

5. Generously apply the dry rub all over the chicken, including under the skin and inside the cavity. Ensure the chicken is well coated with the rub.

6. Place the seasoned whole chicken on the smoker grates, breast-side up.

7. Smoke the chicken at 225°F (107°C) for approximately 2.5 to 3 hours, or until the internal temperature reaches 165°F (74°C) in the thickest part of the breast and thigh when measured with a meat thermometer.

8. Once the chicken reaches the desired internal temperature, remove it from the smoker and transfer it to a cutting board.

Resting:

- Tent the smoked whole chicken loosely with foil and let it rest for about 10-15 minutes before carving. This resting period allows the juices to redistribute, resulting in juicier meat.

Storage Recommendations:

- If you have leftovers, store the carved chicken in an airtight container or wrapped tightly in foil in the refrigerator.

- Consume leftover chicken within 3-4 days for optimal freshness. Reheat gently in the oven or microwave before serving again.

Smoked Beef Ribs

Ingredients:

3-4 pounds (1.4-1.8 kg) beef back ribs
2 tablespoons (30 grams) kosher salt
2 tablespoons (30 grams) black pepper
2 tablespoons (30 grams) garlic powder
1 tablespoon (15 grams) onion powder
1 tablespoon (15 grams) paprika
1 tablespoon (15 grams) brown sugar
1 teaspoon (5 grams) cayenne pepper
Olive oil, for coating

Smoking Process:

1. Preheat your BBQ smoker to 225°F (107°C) using indirect heat.

2. In a small bowl, combine the kosher salt, black pepper, garlic powder, onion powder, paprika, brown sugar, and cayenne pepper to create a dry rub.

3. Pat the beef ribs dry with paper towels and coat them lightly with olive oil.

4. Apply the dry rub generously on all sides of the beef ribs, ensuring an even coating.

5. Place the beef ribs on the smoker grates, bone-side down.

6. Smoke the beef ribs at 225°F (107°C) for approximately 5-6 hours, or until they reach the desired tenderness. They should have a nice bark on the surface and be tender but not falling apart.

7. Once done, remove the beef ribs from the smoker and transfer them to a cutting board or serving platter.

Resting:

- Tent the smoked beef ribs loosely with foil and let them rest for about 10-15 minutes before slicing and serving. This resting period allows the juices to redistribute, resulting in juicier ribs.

Storage Recommendations:

- If you have leftovers, store the smoked beef ribs in an airtight container or wrapped tightly in foil in the refrigerator.

- Consume leftover ribs within 3-4 days for optimal freshness. Reheat gently in the oven or microwave before serving again.

Smoked Pork Shoulder with Sauce

Ingredients:

1 pork shoulder (4-5 pounds / 1.8-2.3 kg)
4 tablespoons (60 grams) brown sugar
2 tablespoons (30 grams) paprika
2 tablespoons (30 grams) garlic powder
2 tablespoons (30 grams) onion powder
1 tablespoon (15 grams) salt
1 tablespoon (15 grams) black pepper
1 teaspoon (5 grams) cayenne pepper
1 cup (240 ml) BBQ sauce of your choice
Olive oil, for coating

Smoking Process:

1. Preheat your BBQ smoker to 225°F (107°C) using indirect heat.

2. In a bowl, combine the brown sugar, paprika, garlic powder, onion powder, salt, black pepper, and cayenne pepper to create a dry rub.

3. Pat the pork shoulder dry with paper towels and coat it lightly with olive oil.

4. Rub the dry seasoning mixture generously all over the pork shoulder, ensuring it's evenly coated.

5. Place the seasoned pork shoulder on the smoker grates, fat-side up.

6. Smoke the pork shoulder at 225°F (107°C) for approximately 1.5 hours per pound (0.45 kg) of meat, or until the internal temperature reaches around 195-205°F (90-96°C) when measured with a meat thermometer inserted into the thickest part of the meat.

7. Once the pork shoulder reaches the desired internal temperature, remove it from the smoker and let it rest.

Resting:

- Tent the smoked pork shoulder loosely with foil and let it rest for about 30-45 minutes before shredding or slicing. This resting period allows the juices to redistribute, resulting in juicier meat.

Sauce:

1. While the pork shoulder is resting, warm the BBQ sauce in a saucepan over low heat.

Serving:

- Shred or slice the smoked pork shoulder and drizzle the warmed BBQ sauce over the meat before serving.

Storage Recommendations:

- If you have leftovers, store the smoked pork shoulder in an airtight container or wrapped tightly in foil in the refrigerator.

- Consume leftover pork within 3-4 days for optimal freshness. Reheat gently in the oven or microwave before serving again.

Smoked Rack of Lamb with Mint Jelly

Ingredients:

2 racks of lamb (about 2 pounds / 0.9 kg each)
Salt and black pepper, to taste
2 tablespoons (30 ml) olive oil
2 tablespoons (30 grams) fresh rosemary, chopped
2 tablespoons (30 grams) fresh thyme, chopped
1 cup (240 ml) mint jelly

Smoking Process:

1. Preheat your BBQ smoker to 225°F (107°C) using indirect heat.

2. Trim excess fat from the racks of lamb, leaving a thin layer for flavor.

3. Season the lamb racks with salt and black pepper, then rub them with olive oil.

4. Sprinkle the chopped fresh rosemary and thyme evenly over the lamb racks, pressing the herbs onto the meat to adhere.

5. Place the seasoned racks of lamb on the smoker grates, bone-side down.

6. Smoke the lamb at 225°F (107°C) for approximately 1.5 to 2 hours, or until the internal temperature reaches around 130-135°F (54-57°C) for medium-rare. Use a meat thermometer for accurate measurement.

7. Once done, remove the racks of lamb from the smoker and let them rest.

Resting:

- Tent the smoked racks of lamb loosely with foil and let them rest for about 15 minutes before slicing. This resting period allows the juices to redistribute, resulting in juicier meat.

Mint Jelly Glaze:

1. While the lamb is resting, warm the mint jelly in a small saucepan over low heat until it becomes a liquid glaze.

2. Brush the mint jelly glaze over the smoked racks of lamb just before serving.

Serving:

- Slice the racks of lamb into individual chops and arrange them on a serving platter.

Storage Recommendations:

- If you have leftovers, store the smoked rack of lamb in an airtight container or wrapped tightly in foil in the refrigerator.

- Consume leftover lamb within 2-3 days for optimal freshness. Reheat gently in the oven before serving again.

Smoked Tofurky

Ingredients:

1 Tofurky Roast (approximately 2 pounds / 0.9 kg)

Smoking Process:

1. Preheat your BBQ smoker to 225°F (107°C) using indirect heat.

2. Remove the Tofurky Roast from its packaging and place it directly onto the smoker grates.

3. Smoke the Tofurky Roast at 225°F (107°C) for approximately 1.5 to 2 hours, or until it has absorbed some smoky flavor and has a slightly firmer texture.

4. Once done, remove the Tofurky Roast from the smoker and let it rest.

Resting:

- Allow the smoked Tofurky Roast to rest for about 10-15 minutes before slicing or serving. This resting period helps the flavors settle and enhances the texture.

Storage Recommendations:

- If you have leftovers, store the smoked Tofurky Roast in an airtight container or wrapped tightly in foil in the refrigerator.

- Consume leftover Tofurky within 3-4 days for optimal freshness. Reheat gently in the oven or microwave before serving again.

Smoked Portobello Mushrooms with Balsamic Glaze

Ingredients:

4 large Portobello mushrooms
1/4 cup (60 ml) balsamic vinegar
2 tablespoons (30 ml) olive oil
Salt and black pepper, to taste
Fresh parsley, chopped (for garnish)

Smoking Process:

1. Preheat your BBQ smoker to 225°F (107°C) using indirect heat.

2. Gently clean the Portobello mushrooms using a damp cloth or paper towel to remove any dirt. Remove the stems if desired.

3. In a small bowl, mix together the balsamic vinegar and olive oil.

4. Lightly brush both sides of the Portobello mushrooms with the balsamic and olive oil mixture. Season with salt and black pepper.

5. Place the mushrooms directly on the smoker grates, gill-side down.

6. Smoke the Portobello mushrooms at 225°F (107°C) for approximately 30-40 minutes, or until they have a tender texture and have absorbed some of the smoky flavor.

7. Once done, remove the mushrooms from the smoker and let them rest.

Resting:

- Allow the smoked Portobello mushrooms to rest for about 5 minutes before serving.

Finishing:

- Optionally, drizzle the smoked Portobello mushrooms with a bit more balsamic glaze before serving.
- Garnish with chopped fresh parsley for added flavor and presentation.

Storage Recommendations:

- If you have leftovers, store the smoked Portobello mushrooms in an airtight container in the refrigerator.
- Consume leftover mushrooms within 2-3 days for optimal freshness. Reheat gently in the oven or microwave before serving again.

Smoked Stuffed Bell Peppers

Ingredients:

4 large bell peppers
1 cup (200g) cooked rice
1 can (15 oz / 425g) black beans, drained and rinsed
1 cup (150g) corn kernels (fresh, canned, or frozen)
1 cup (150g) diced tomatoes
1 cup (100g) shredded cheese (cheddar, mozzarella, or your choice)
1/2 cup (75g) diced onion
2 cloves garlic, minced
1 teaspoon (5ml) olive oil
Salt and pepper, to taste
Fresh parsley or cilantro, chopped (for garnish)

Smoking Process:

1. Preheat your BBQ smoker to 225°F (107°C) using indirect heat.

2. Cut the tops off the bell peppers and remove the seeds and membranes.

3. In a skillet over medium heat, add olive oil. Sauté the diced onion and minced garlic until softened.

4. In a mixing bowl, combine the cooked rice, black beans, corn kernels, diced tomatoes, sautéed onion and garlic mixture, and shredded cheese. Mix well. Season with salt and pepper to taste.

5. Stuff the hollowed bell peppers with the rice and vegetable mixture.

6. Place the stuffed bell peppers on the smoker grates.

7. Smoke the stuffed bell peppers at 225°F (107°C) for approximately 1.5 to 2 hours, or until the peppers have softened and the filling is heated through.

8. Once done, remove the stuffed bell peppers from the smoker and let them rest.

Resting:

- Allow the smoked stuffed bell peppers to rest for about 5-10 minutes before serving.

Finishing:

- Garnish the stuffed bell peppers with chopped fresh parsley or cilantro for added freshness.

Storage Recommendations:

- If you have leftovers, store the smoked stuffed bell peppers in an airtight container in the refrigerator.

- Consume leftover stuffed peppers within 2-3 days for optimal freshness. Reheat gently in the oven or microwave before serving again.

SIDE DISHES

Mac and Cheese

Ingredients:

1 pound (450g) elbow macaroni
1/2 cup (115g) unsalted butter
1/2 cup (60g) all-purpose flour
4 cups (950ml) whole milk
2 cups (200g) shredded sharp cheddar cheese
1 cup (100g) shredded Gruyère cheese
1 cup (100g) shredded mozzarella cheese
1/2 cup (50g) grated Parmesan cheese
1 teaspoon (5ml) Dijon mustard
1/2 teaspoon (2.5ml) smoked paprika
Salt and pepper, to taste
Cooking spray or butter (for greasing)

Smoking Process:

1. Preheat your BBQ smoker to 225°F (107°C) using indirect heat.

2. Cook the elbow macaroni according to the package instructions until al dente. Drain and set aside.

3. In a large saucepan over medium heat, melt the butter. Add the flour and whisk continuously for about 2 minutes to create a roux.

4. Gradually pour in the whole milk while whisking constantly to avoid lumps. Cook the mixture for about 5-7 minutes until it thickens, stirring frequently.

5. Reduce the heat to low. Add the shredded cheddar, Gruyère, mozzarella, and grated Parmesan cheese to the saucepan. Stir until the cheese melts and the sauce is smooth.

6. Stir in the Dijon mustard and smoked paprika. Season with salt and pepper to taste.

7. Add the cooked elbow macaroni into the cheese sauce, stirring until the macaroni is well coated.

8. Grease a large disposable aluminum pan or a cast-iron skillet with cooking spray or butter.

9. Transfer the macaroni and cheese mixture to the greased pan or skillet.

10. Place the pan or skillet on the smoker grates.

11. Smoke the mac and cheese at 225°F (107°C) for approximately 1 hour, or until it develops a smoky flavor and the top forms a golden crust.

12. Once done, remove the smoked mac and cheese from the smoker and let it rest.

Resting:

- Allow the smoked mac and cheese to rest for about 10-15 minutes before serving.

Storage Recommendations:

- If you have leftovers, store the smoked mac and cheese in an airtight container in the refrigerator.

- Consume leftover mac and cheese within 3-4 days for optimal freshness. Reheat gently in the oven or microwave before serving again.

Brussels Sprouts with Bacon

Ingredients:

2 pounds (900g) Brussels sprouts, trimmed and halved
8 slices bacon, chopped
2 tablespoons (30ml) olive oil
Salt and pepper, to taste
1 teaspoon (5ml) garlic powder
1 teaspoon (5ml) smoked paprika

Smoking Process:

1. Preheat your BBQ smoker to 225°F (107°C) using indirect heat.

2. In a large bowl, toss the halved Brussels sprouts with olive oil, salt, pepper, garlic powder, and smoked paprika until evenly coated.

3. Spread the seasoned Brussels sprouts on a baking sheet or aluminum pan.

4. Sprinkle the chopped bacon evenly over the Brussels sprouts.

5. Place the baking sheet or pan of Brussels sprouts and bacon on the smoker grates.

6. Smoke the Brussels sprouts and bacon at 225°F (107°C) for approximately 1 to 1.5 hours, or until the Brussels sprouts are tender and the bacon is crispy, stirring occasionally for even cooking.

7. Once done, remove the smoked Brussels sprouts and bacon from the smoker.

Resting:

- Allow the smoked Brussels sprouts and bacon to rest for about 5 minutes before serving.

Storage Recommendations:

- If you have leftovers, store the smoked Brussels sprouts and bacon in an airtight container in the refrigerator.

- Consume leftover Brussels sprouts within 2-3 days for optimal freshness. Reheat gently in the oven or microwave before serving again

Corn on the Cob with Garlic Butter

Ingredients:

6 ears of corn
1/2 cup (115g) unsalted butter, softened
2 cloves garlic, minced
Salt and pepper, to taste
Fresh parsley, chopped (for garnish)

Smoking Process:

1. Preheat your BBQ smoker to 225°F (107°C) using indirect heat.

2. Peel back the husks of the corn without removing them entirely. Remove the silk strands and then pull the husks back up to cover the corn.

3. Place the prepared ears of corn directly on the smoker grates.

4. Smoke the corn at 225°F (107°C) for approximately 45 minutes to 1 hour, or until the kernels are tender and slightly charred, turning the corn occasionally for even cooking.

5. While the corn is smoking, prepare the garlic butter. In a small bowl, mix the softened butter with minced garlic, salt, and pepper until well combined.

6. Once the corn is done, remove it from the smoker.

Resting:

- Allow the smoked corn to rest for about 5 minutes.

Finishing:

1. Peel back the husks and brush each ear of corn generously with the garlic butter mixture.

2. Garnish the corn with chopped fresh parsley for added flavor and presentation.

Storage Recommendations:

- If you have leftovers, store the smoked corn in an airtight container in the refrigerator.

- Consume leftover corn within 1-2 days for optimal freshness. Reheat gently in the oven or microwave before serving again.

Potato Salad

Ingredients:

2 pounds (900g) potatoes, preferably red or Yukon gold
1/2 cup (120ml) mayonnaise
2 tablespoons (30ml) apple cider vinegar
1 tablespoon (15ml) Dijon mustard
1/4 cup (15g) fresh parsley, chopped
2 green onions, thinly sliced
Salt and black pepper, to taste
1 teaspoon (5ml) garlic powder
1 teaspoon (5ml) smoked paprika
Cooking oil (for coating potatoes)

Smoking Process:

1. Preheat your BBQ smoker to 225°F (107°C) using indirect heat.

2. Wash and scrub the potatoes thoroughly. Pat them dry and then coat them lightly with cooking oil.

3. Place the whole potatoes directly on the smoker grates.

4. Smoke the potatoes at 225°F (107°C) for approximately 1.5 to 2 hours or until they are tender when pierced with a fork. The timing will vary depending on the size of the potatoes.

5. Once done, remove the smoked potatoes from the smoker and let them rest until they are cool enough to handle.

Resting:

- Let the smoked potatoes cool for about 10-15 minutes.

Assembling the Salad:

1. Cut the smoked potatoes into bite-sized chunks and place them in a large mixing bowl.

2. In a separate bowl, mix the mayonnaise, apple cider vinegar, Dijon mustard, chopped parsley, sliced green onions, salt, black pepper, garlic powder, and smoked paprika until well combined.

3. Pour the dressing mixture over the smoked potatoes and gently toss until the potatoes are evenly coated.

4. Adjust seasoning to taste if needed.

5. Chill the smoked potato salad in the refrigerator for at least an hour before serving to allow the flavors to meld.

Storage Recommendations:

- Store any leftover smoked potato salad in an airtight container in the refrigerator.

- Consume the leftover salad within 2-3 days for optimal freshness. Mix gently before serving again.

Baked Beans

Ingredients:

2 cans (15 oz / 425g each) navy beans or any preferred beans
1/2 cup (120ml) ketchup
1/4 cup (60ml) molasses
1/4 cup (60ml) maple syrup
1/4 cup (60ml) apple cider vinegar
1 small onion, finely diced
4 slices bacon, chopped
2 tablespoons (30g) brown sugar
1 tablespoon (15g) mustard
1 teaspoon (5ml) Worcestershire sauce
Salt and pepper, to taste

Smoking Process:

1. Preheat your BBQ smoker to 225°F (107°C) using indirect heat.

2. In a cast-iron skillet or disposable aluminum pan, combine the beans (drained and rinsed if using canned beans), ketchup, molasses, maple syrup, apple cider

vinegar, diced onion, chopped bacon, brown sugar, mustard, Worcestershire sauce, salt, and pepper. Mix well.

3. Place the skillet or pan of baked bean mixture on the smoker grates.

4. Smoke the beans at 225°F (107°C) for approximately 2 to 2.5 hours, stirring occasionally, until the flavors meld together and the beans have absorbed the smoky essence.

5. Once done, remove the smoked baked beans from the smoker.

Resting:

- Allow the smoked baked beans to rest for about 5-10 minutes before serving.

Storage Recommendations:

- Store any leftover smoked baked beans in an airtight container in the refrigerator.

- Consume leftover beans within 3-4 days for optimal freshness. Reheat gently in the microwave or on the stovetop before serving again

Asparagus with Lemon and Parmesan

Ingredients:

1 pound (450g) asparagus spears, trimmed
2 tablespoons (30ml) olive oil
Zest of 1 lemon
1/4 cup (20g) grated Parmesan cheese
Salt and pepper, to taste
Lemon wedges (for serving)
Fresh parsley, chopped (for garnish)

Smoking Process:

1. Preheat your BBQ smoker to 225°F (107°C) using indirect heat.

2. Place the trimmed asparagus spears in a single layer on a baking sheet or a grill pan.

3. Drizzle the asparagus with olive oil and sprinkle with lemon zest, grated Parmesan cheese, salt, and pepper. Toss gently to coat the asparagus evenly.

4. Place the baking sheet or grill pan of asparagus directly on the smoker grates.

5. Smoke the asparagus at 225°F (107°C) for approximately 20-25 minutes, or until they are tender yet still slightly crisp, with a touch of smokiness.

6. Once done, remove the smoked asparagus from the smoker.

Resting:

- Allow the smoked asparagus to rest for about 5 minutes before serving.

Finishing:

- Serve the smoked asparagus with lemon wedges on the side for additional zest and a sprinkle of chopped fresh parsley for garnish.

Storage Recommendations:

- If you have leftovers, store the smoked asparagus in an airtight container in the refrigerator.

- Consume leftover asparagus within 2-3 days for optimal freshness. Reheat gently in the oven or microwave before serving again.

Collard Greens

Ingredients:

2 pounds (900g) collard greens, stems removed and leaves chopped
6 slices bacon, chopped
1 onion, finely chopped
3 cloves garlic, minced
4 cups (950ml) chicken or vegetable broth
1 teaspoon (5ml) apple cider vinegar
Salt and pepper, to taste
Crushed red pepper flakes (optional, for heat)

Smoking Process:

1. Preheat your BBQ smoker to 225°F (107°C) using indirect heat.

2. In a large Dutch oven or a sturdy disposable aluminum pan, cook the chopped bacon over medium heat until it becomes crispy.

3. Add the finely chopped onion to the bacon and cook until the onion becomes translucent, stirring occasionally.

4. Stir in the minced garlic and cook for an additional minute until fragrant.

5. Add the chopped collard greens to the pan and pour in the chicken or vegetable broth.

6. Season the collard greens with salt, pepper, and optionally crushed red pepper flakes for heat. Stir well to combine.

7. Cover the pan with a lid or tightly with aluminum foil.

8. Place the covered pan of collard greens directly on the smoker grates.

9. Smoke the collard greens at 225°F (107°C) for approximately 2.5 to 3 hours, or until they are tender, stirring occasionally for even cooking.

10. Once done, remove the smoked collard greens from the smoker.

Resting:

- Allow the smoked collard greens to rest for about 5-10 minutes before serving.

Storage Recommendations:

- Store any leftover smoked collard greens in an airtight container in the refrigerator.

- Consume leftover greens within 3-4 days for optimal freshness. Reheat gently in the microwave or on the stovetop before serving again.

Sweet Potato Casserole

Ingredients:

4 large sweet potatoes (about 2 pounds / 900g), peeled and cubed
1/2 cup (115g) unsalted butter, melted
1/4 cup (60ml) maple syrup
2 large eggs, beaten
1/4 cup (60ml) milk
1 teaspoon (5ml) vanilla extract
1/2 cup (100g) brown sugar
1/3 cup (40g) all-purpose flour
1/2 cup (65g) chopped pecans
1/2 teaspoon (2.5ml) ground cinnamon
Pinch of salt

Smoking Process:

1. Preheat your BBQ smoker to 225°F (107°C) using indirect heat.

2. Place the peeled and cubed sweet potatoes in a disposable aluminum pan or a heatproof dish suitable for smoking.

3. Smoke the sweet potatoes at 225°F (107°C) for approximately 2 to 2.5 hours, or until they are tender and have absorbed a smoky flavor.

4. Once the sweet potatoes are done, remove them from the smoker and let them cool for a few minutes.

Resting:

- Allow the smoked sweet potatoes to rest for about 10-15 minutes.

Assembling the Casserole:

1. Preheat your oven to 350°F (175°C).

2. In a large mixing bowl, mash the smoked sweet potatoes.

3. Add the melted butter, maple syrup, beaten eggs, milk, and vanilla extract to the mashed sweet potatoes. Mix until well combined.

4. In a separate bowl, combine the brown sugar, flour, chopped pecans, ground cinnamon, and a pinch of salt.

5. Spread the sweet potato mixture evenly into a baking dish and sprinkle the topping mixture over the sweet potatoes.

6. Place the baking dish in the preheated oven and bake for approximately 25-30 minutes, or until the topping is golden brown and the casserole is heated through.

7. Once done, remove the casserole from the oven.

Storage Recommendations:

- Store any leftover smoked sweet potato casserole in an airtight container in the refrigerator.

- Consume leftover casserole within 3-4 days for optimal freshness. Reheat in the oven or microwave before serving again.

Cabbage Steaks

Ingredients:

1 head of cabbage
Olive oil (for brushing)
Salt and pepper, to taste
Optional: Seasonings of choice like garlic powder, smoked paprika, or onion powder

Smoking Process:

1. Preheat your BBQ smoker to 225°F (107°C) using indirect heat.

2. Remove any loose or damaged outer leaves from the cabbage. Cut the cabbage into thick slices, about 1-inch (2.5cm) thick, creating "steaks." Ensure the core holds each slice together.

3. Brush both sides of the cabbage steaks lightly with olive oil.

4. Season the cabbage steaks with salt, pepper, and any optional seasonings of your choice, ensuring an even coating on both sides.

5. Place the cabbage steaks directly on the smoker grates.

6. Smoke the cabbage steaks at 225°F (107°C) for approximately 45 minutes to 1 hour, or until they are tender and have a light smoky flavor. Flip the steaks halfway through the smoking process for even cooking.

7. Once done, remove the smoked cabbage steaks from the smoker.

Resting:

- Allow the smoked cabbage steaks to rest for about 5-10 minutes before serving.

Storage Recommendations:

- Store any leftover smoked cabbage steaks in an airtight container in the refrigerator.

- Consume leftover cabbage within 2-3 days for optimal freshness. Reheat gently in the oven or microwave before serving again.

Veggie Skewers

Ingredients:

2 zucchinis
2 bell peppers (any color)
1 red onion
1 pint (300g) cherry tomatoes
8-10 wooden skewers, soaked in water for 30 minutes

Smoking Process:

1. Preheat your BBQ smoker to 225°F (107°C) using indirect heat.

2. Cut the zucchinis into thick slices. Deseed and cut the bell peppers and red onion into chunks, roughly the same size as the zucchini slices.

3. Thread the vegetables onto the soaked wooden skewers, alternating between zucchini slices, bell pepper chunks, onion pieces, and cherry tomatoes until the skewers are filled.

4. Place the assembled skewers directly on the smoker grates.

5. Smoke the veggie skewers at 225°F (107°C) for approximately 25-30 minutes, turning them occasionally to ensure even cooking and a light smoky flavor.

6. Once done, remove the smoked veggie skewers from the smoker.

Resting:

- Allow the smoked veggie skewers to rest for about 5 minutes before serving.

Storage Recommendations:

- Store any leftover smoked veggie skewers in an airtight container in the refrigerator.

- Consume leftover skewers within 2-3 days for optimal freshness. Reheat gently in the oven or microwave before serving again.

DESSERTS

Peach Cobbler

Ingredients:

6-8 ripe peaches, peeled, pitted, and sliced
1 cup (200g) granulated sugar
1 tablespoon (15ml) lemon juice
1 teaspoon (5ml) vanilla extract
1/2 cup (115g) unsalted butter, melted
1 cup (120g) all-purpose flour
1 teaspoon (5g) baking powder
1/2 teaspoon (2.5g) salt
1 cup (240ml) milk
Ground cinnamon (optional, for sprinkling)

Smoking Process:

1. Preheat your BBQ smoker to 375°F (190°C) using indirect heat.

2. In a bowl, combine the sliced peaches, granulated sugar, lemon juice, and vanilla extract. Toss gently until the peaches are coated evenly.

3. Place the peach mixture into a baking dish or a disposable aluminum pan.

4. In another bowl, mix the melted butter, flour, baking powder, salt, and milk until it forms a smooth batter.

5. Pour the batter over the peach mixture in the baking dish, spreading it evenly.

6. Place the baking dish on the smoker grates.

7. Smoke the peach cobbler at 375°F (190°C) for approximately 45-55 minutes, or until the top is golden brown and the cobbler is bubbling around the edges.

8. Once done, remove the smoked peach cobbler from the smoker.

Resting:

- Allow the smoked peach cobbler to rest for about 10-15 minutes before serving.

Storage Recommendations:

- Store any leftover peach cobbler in an airtight container in the refrigerator.

- Consume leftover cobbler within 2-3 days for optimal freshness. Reheat gently in the oven before serving again.

Chocolate Pecan Pie

Ingredients:

1 9-inch (23cm) pie crust, unbaked
1 cup (240ml) corn syrup
1 cup (200g) granulated sugar
3 large eggs
1 teaspoon (5ml) vanilla extract
2 tablespoons (30ml) unsalted butter, melted
1 cup (120g) pecan halves
1 cup (175g) semi-sweet chocolate chips

Smoking Process:

1. Preheat your BBQ smoker to 350°F (175°C) using indirect heat.

2. Place the unbaked pie crust in a pie dish.

3. In a mixing bowl, combine the corn syrup, granulated sugar, eggs, vanilla extract, and melted butter. Mix until well combined.

4. Stir in the pecan halves and chocolate chips into the syrup mixture.

5. Pour the mixture into the unbaked pie crust.

6. Place the pie dish onto the smoker grates.

7. Smoke the pecan pie at 350°F (175°C) for approximately 45-55 minutes or until the filling is set and slightly puffed.

8. Once done, remove the smoked chocolate pecan pie from the smoker.

Resting:

- Allow the smoked pecan pie to rest and cool for at least an hour before slicing.

Storage Recommendations:

- Store any leftover pecan pie in the refrigerator, covered with plastic wrap or placed in an airtight container.

- Consume leftover pie within 2-3 days for optimal freshness. Serve chilled or slightly warmed in the oven before serving again.

Banana Split to Share (Maybe)

Ingredients:

9 ripe bananas
1/2 cup (60g) brown sugar
3 tablespoons (30g) unsalted butter, melted
2 teaspoon (5ml) vanilla extract
2/3 teaspoon (2.5g) ground cinnamon
Vanilla ice cream
Chocolate syrup, for drizzling
Whipped cream
Marshmallows (optional, for garnish)
Chopped nuts (optional, for topping)

Smoking Process:

1. Preheat your BBQ smoker to 350°F (175°C) using indirect heat.

2. In a small bowl, mix the brown sugar, melted butter, vanilla extract, and ground cinnamon to create a glaze.

3. Leave the bananas in their peels and make a lengthwise slit along the inside curve of each banana, leaving the peel intact. Be careful not to cut through the bottom peel.

4. Gently pull open the slit and stuff each banana with the prepared glaze mixture.

5. Place the stuffed bananas directly on the smoker grates.

6. Smoke the bananas at 350°F (175°C) for approximately 10-15 minutes or until the bananas are soft and the glaze is bubbling.

7. Once done, remove the smoked bananas from the smoker.

Resting:

- Allow the smoked bananas to cool for a few minutes.

Assembling the Banana Split:

1. Carefully peel open the top of each banana and place 4 on a serving dish.

2. Scoop vanilla ice cream along the bananas and drizzle chocolate syrup generously before placing three more on top, add more ice cream and drizzle again with chocolate syrup, repeat with the remaining bananas to form a triangle.

3. Garnish with a dollop of whipped cream, marshmallows (if using), and chopped nuts (if desired).

Storage Recommendations:

- It's best to enjoy banana splits immediately after preparation. Leftovers may not store well due to the melting ice cream and toppings. If needed, store any remaining banana splits in the freezer, but be aware that the texture may change upon thawing.

Apple Crisp

Ingredients:

6 cups (about 6 medium-sized) apples, peeled, cored, and sliced into wedges
1 tablespoon (15ml) lemon juice
1/2 cup (100g) granulated sugar
2 tablespoons (15g) all-purpose flour
1 teaspoon (2g) ground cinnamon
1/4 teaspoon (0.5g) ground nutmeg
1 cup (100g) rolled oats
1/2 cup (100g) brown sugar
1/3 cup (40g) all-purpose flour
1/3 cup (75g) unsalted butter, softened
Vanilla ice cream (optional, for serving)

Smoking Process:

1. Preheat your BBQ smoker to 350°F (175°C) using indirect heat.

2. In a large mixing bowl, toss the sliced apples with lemon juice to prevent browning.

3. Add granulated sugar, 2 tablespoons of flour, ground cinnamon, and ground nutmeg to the apples. Mix until the apples are evenly coated.

4. In another bowl, combine rolled oats, brown sugar, 1/3 cup of flour, and softened butter. Mix until it forms a crumbly texture.

5. Spread the oat mixture evenly in a baking dish suitable for smoking.

6. Arrange the apple wedges evenly around the baking dish, gently pushing into the mixture so they stand proud of the crispy base

7. Place the baking dish onto the smoker grates.

8. Smoke the apple crisp at 350°F (175°C) for about 45-55 minutes, or until the apples are tender and the top is golden brown.

9. Once done, remove the smoked apple crisp from the smoker.

Resting:

- Allow the smoked apple crisp to rest for about 10-15 minutes before serving.

Serving and Storage Recommendations:

- Serve the smoked apple crisp warm, optionally topped with vanilla ice cream.
- Store any leftover apple crisp in an airtight container in the refrigerator. Reheat gently in the oven before serving again. Enjoy within a few days for the best taste and texture.

Cherry Cheesecake

Ingredients:

For the Crust:

1 1/2 cups (150g) graham cracker crumbs
1/4 cup (50g) granulated sugar
1/2 cup (115g) unsalted butter, melted

For the Filling:

24 ounces (680g) cream cheese, softened
1 cup (200g) granulated sugar
4 large eggs
1 teaspoon (5ml) vanilla extract
1 cup (240ml) sour cream

For the Cherry Topping:

1 can (300g) red or black cherries, pitted
12 fresh cherries with stems

1/2 cup (100g) granulated sugar
1 tablespoon (15ml) lemon juice
1 tablespoon (8g) cornstarch
2 tablespoons (30ml) water

Smoking Process:

1. Preheat your BBQ smoker to 325°F (163°C) using indirect heat.

2. Mix the graham cracker crumbs, 1/4 cup sugar, and melted butter in a bowl until combined. Press the mixture firmly onto the bottom of a springform pan to form the crust.

3. In a large mixing bowl, beat the cream cheese and 1 cup sugar until smooth. Add eggs one at a time, mixing well after each addition. Stir in the vanilla extract and sour cream until thoroughly combined.

4. Pour the cream cheese filling onto the prepared crust in the springform pan.

5. Wrap the bottom of the springform pan in aluminum foil for protection, ensuring the foil comes over halfway up the sides of the pan and place it in a larger pan or baking dish filled with water to create a water bath for even baking. Place it on the smoker grates.

6. Smoke the cheesecake at 325°F (163°C) for about 1 hour and 15 minutes, or until the edges are set and the center is slightly jiggly.

7. While the cheesecake is smoking, prepare the cherry topping. In a saucepan over medium heat, combine the canned cherries, 1/2 cup sugar, and lemon juice. In a separate bowl, mix cornstarch and water, then add to the cherry mixture. Cook until thickened, stirring frequently. Add the fresh cherries and remove from heat to let it cool.

8. Once the cheesecake is done, turn off the smoker but leave the cheesecake inside for another 30 minutes to an hour to cool gradually.

9. After cooling, spread the cherry topping evenly over the cheesecake.

Resting:

- Refrigerate the smoked cherry cheesecake for at least 4 hours, or preferably overnight, before serving. Top with freshly whipped cream or vanilla ice cream.

Storage Recommendations:

- Store any leftover cherry cheesecake in the refrigerator, covered with plastic wrap or placed in an airtight container. Consume within 3-4 days for the best taste and texture.

Pineapple Upside-Down Cake

Ingredients:

For the Topping:

1/2 cup (115g) unsalted butter, melted
3/4 cup (150g) brown sugar
1 can (20 ounces / 565g) pineapple slices, drained
Maraschino cherries (optional), drained

For the Cake Batter:

1 1/2 cups (190g) all-purpose flour
3/4 cup (150g) granulated sugar
2 teaspoons (8g) baking powder
1/4 teaspoon (1.25g) salt
1/2 cup (120ml) milk
1/4 cup (60ml) pineapple juice (reserved from the canned pineapple)
1/4 cup (60g) unsalted butter, melted
1 teaspoon (5ml) vanilla extract
1 large egg

Smoking Process:

1. Preheat your BBQ smoker to 350°F (175°C) using indirect heat.
2. In a bowl, combine the melted butter and brown sugar. Spread this mixture evenly in the bottom of a cake pan or a cast-iron skillet.
3. Place pineapple slices on top of the butter-sugar mixture. Optionally, place maraschino cherries in the centers of the pineapple slices.
4. In a separate bowl, mix the flour, granulated sugar, baking powder, and salt.
5. Add the milk, reserved pineapple juice, melted butter, vanilla extract, and egg into the dry ingredients. Mix until the batter is smooth.
6. Carefully pour the cake batter over the arranged pineapple slices in the pan.
7. Place the cake pan or skillet onto the smoker grates.
8. Smoke the pineapple upside-down cake at 350°F (175°C) for about 35-45 minutes or until a toothpick inserted into the center comes out clean.
9. Once done, remove the cake from the smoker.

Resting:

- Allow the cake to cool in the pan for 10-15 minutes.
- Carefully invert the cake onto a serving plate, releasing it from the pan. Let it rest for a few more minutes before serving.

Storage Recommendations:

- Store any leftover pineapple upside-down cake covered in the refrigerator. Reheat individual slices in the microwave or oven before serving. Enjoy within 2-3 days for the best taste and texture.

Pumpkin Pie

Ingredients:

For the Pie Filling:

1 3/4 cups (425g) pumpkin puree
1 cup (240ml) evaporated milk
1/2 cup (100g) granulated sugar
2 large eggs
1 teaspoon (5ml) vanilla extract
1 teaspoon (2g) ground cinnamon
1/2 teaspoon (1g) ground ginger
1/4 teaspoon (0.5g) ground nutmeg
1/4 teaspoon (0.5g) ground cloves
1/4 teaspoon (1g) salt

For the Pie Crust:

1 1/4 cups (155g) all-purpose flour
1/2 teaspoon (2.5g) salt
1/3 cup (75g) unsalted butter, chilled and diced

2-3 tablespoons (30-45ml) ice water

Smoking Process:

1. Preheat your BBQ smoker to 350°F (175°C) using indirect heat.

2. In a large bowl, mix the flour and salt for the pie crust. Add the chilled diced butter and work it into the flour until it resembles coarse crumbs. Gradually add ice water, one tablespoon at a time, and mix until the dough comes together. Form the dough into a disc, cover it with plastic wrap, and refrigerate for 30 minutes.

3. Roll out the chilled dough on a floured surface to fit a 9-inch pie dish. Transfer the rolled-out dough to the pie dish, trim the edges, and crimp or flute as desired.

4. In another bowl, whisk together the pumpkin puree, evaporated milk, granulated sugar, eggs, vanilla extract, ground cinnamon, ground ginger, ground nutmeg, ground cloves, and salt until well combined.

5. Pour the pumpkin mixture into the prepared pie crust.

6. Place the pie onto the smoker grates.

7. Smoke the pumpkin pie at 350°F (175°C) for approximately 45-55 minutes or until the center is set (a toothpick inserted near the center should come out clean).

8. Once done, remove the pie from the smoker.

Resting:

- Allow the pumpkin pie to cool completely at room temperature, then refrigerate it for at least 2-3 hours or overnight before serving. For extra charm, heat a small wire rack in the smoker and use a brand to score the pumpkin topping.

Storage Recommendations:

- Store any leftover pumpkin pie in the refrigerator, covered with plastic wrap, or placed in an airtight container. Enjoy within 2-3 days for the best taste and texture.

Mixed Berry Galette

Ingredients:

For the Galette Dough:

1 1/4 cups (155g) all-purpose flour
1 tablespoon (12g) granulated sugar
1/4 teaspoon (1g) salt
1/2 cup (115g) unsalted butter, chilled and diced
3-4 tablespoons (45-60ml) ice water

For the Filling:

2 cups (300g) mixed berries (such as strawberries, blueberries, raspberries, blackberries)
1/4 cup (50g) granulated sugar
2 tablespoons (15g) cornstarch
1 tablespoon (15ml) lemon juice
Zest of 1 lemon
1 tablespoon (15ml) milk (for brushing)
1 tablespoon (12g) coarse sugar (for sprinkling)

Smoking Process:

1. Preheat your BBQ smoker to 375°F (190°C) using indirect heat.

2. For the galette dough, in a large bowl, mix the flour, sugar, and salt. Add the chilled diced butter and work it into the flour until it resembles coarse crumbs. Gradually add ice water, one tablespoon at a time, and mix until the dough comes together. Form the dough into a disc, cover it with plastic wrap, and refrigerate for 30 minutes.

3. In a separate bowl, gently toss the mixed berries with sugar, cornstarch, lemon juice, and lemon zest until the berries are evenly coated.

4. Roll out the chilled dough on a floured surface into a rough circle, about 12 inches in diameter.

5. Place the rolled-out dough onto a parchment-lined baking sheet.

6. Arrange the mixed berry filling in the center of the dough, leaving a border around the edges.

7. Carefully fold the edges of the dough over the berries, pleating as you go, to create the galette shape. Press lightly to seal any cracks.

8. Brush the edges of the dough with milk and sprinkle the coarse sugar over the edges.

9. Place the baking sheet with the galette onto the smoker grates.

10. Smoke the mixed berry galette at 375°F (190°C) for approximately 35-45 minutes or until the crust is golden and the filling is bubbling.

11. Once done, remove the galette from the smoker.

Resting:

- Allow the galette to cool for at least 15-20 minutes before slicing and serving. Top with Vanilla ice cream

Storage Recommendations:

- Store any leftover mixed berry galette in the refrigerator, covered with plastic wrap or placed in an airtight container. Reheat individual slices in the microwave or oven before serving. Enjoy within 2-3 days for the best taste and texture.

Bread Pudding

Ingredients:

6 cups (360g) bread cubes (stale bread works well)
2 cups (480ml) whole milk
1/2 cup (120ml) heavy cream
4 large eggs
1/2 cup (100g) granulated sugar
1/4 cup (50g) brown sugar
2 teaspoons (10ml) vanilla extract
1/2 teaspoon (2.5g) ground cinnamon
1/4 teaspoon (0.5g) ground nutmeg
1/4 teaspoon (1g) salt
1/2 cup (75g) raisins or dried fruit (optional)
1/2 cup (60g) chopped nuts (optional)
2 tablespoons (30g) unsalted butter, melted

Smoking Process:

1. Preheat your BBQ smoker to 350°F (175°C) using indirect heat.

2. In a large bowl, combine the milk, heavy cream, eggs, granulated sugar, brown sugar, vanilla extract, ground cinnamon, ground nutmeg, and salt. Whisk until well combined.

3. Add the bread cubes to the milk mixture. Gently fold until all the bread cubes are coated and soaked in the mixture. Let it sit for 10-15 minutes to allow the bread to absorb the liquid.

4. If using, fold in the raisins or dried fruit and chopped nuts into the bread mixture.

5. Transfer the bread pudding mixture into a greased baking dish.

6. Drizzle the melted butter over the top of the bread pudding.

7. Place the baking dish onto the smoker grates.

8. Smoke the bread pudding at 350°F (175°C) for about 45-55 minutes or until the top is golden brown and the pudding is set.

9. Once done, remove the bread pudding from the smoker.

Resting:

- Allow the bread pudding to cool for about 10-15 minutes before serving.

Storage Recommendations:

- Store any leftover bread pudding covered in the refrigerator. Reheat individual portions in the microwave or oven before serving. Enjoy within 2-3 days for the best taste and texture.

Chocolate Fondue

Ingredients:

8 ounces (225g) semi-sweet chocolate, chopped
1 cup (240ml) heavy cream
1 teaspoon (5ml) vanilla extract
Assorted fruits (strawberries, bananas, apples), marshmallows, pretzels, or pound cake for dipping

Smoking Process:

1. Preheat your BBQ smoker to 250°F (120°C) using indirect heat.

2. In a heatproof bowl that is smoker-safe, combine the chopped semi-sweet chocolate and heavy cream.

3. Place the bowl on the smoker grates.

4. Let the chocolate and cream heat together, stirring occasionally, until the chocolate is melted and the mixture is smooth and well combined. This might take approximately 20-25 minutes.

5. Once melted and smooth, remove the bowl from the smoker.

Resting:

- Allow the chocolate fondue to cool slightly for a few minutes before serving.

Storage Recommendations:

- Leftover chocolate fondue can be stored in an airtight container in the refrigerator for up to 2-3 days. Reheat gently using a microwave or stovetop until smooth before serving again.

SAUCES AND CONDIMENTS

Homemade BBQ Sauce

Ingredients:

1 cup (240ml) ketchup
1/2 cup (120ml) apple cider vinegar
1/4 cup (60ml) water
1/4 cup (60g) brown sugar
2 tablespoons (30ml) Worcestershire sauce
2 tablespoons (30ml) molasses
1 tablespoon (15ml) Dijon mustard
1 teaspoon (5ml) smoked paprika
1 teaspoon (5ml) garlic powder
1 teaspoon (5ml) onion powder
1/2 teaspoon (2.5ml) ground black pepper
1/2 teaspoon (2.5ml) salt
1/4 teaspoon (1.25ml) cayenne pepper (adjust to taste for spice)

Smoking Process:

1. Preheat your BBQ smoker to 225°F (107°C) using indirect heat.

2. In a saucepan, combine all the ingredients - ketchup, apple cider vinegar, water, brown sugar, Worcestershire sauce, molasses, Dijon mustard, smoked paprika, garlic powder, onion powder, black pepper, salt, and cayenne pepper.

3. Place the saucepan on the smoker grates.

4. Simmer the sauce, stirring occasionally, for about 1 hour to allow the flavors to meld and the sauce to thicken slightly.

5. Once the sauce has reached the desired consistency and flavors have developed, remove the saucepan from the smoker.

Resting:

- Allow the homemade BBQ sauce to cool completely before transferring it to an airtight container or jar.

Storage Recommendations:

- Store the leftover BBQ sauce in a sealed container in the refrigerator for up to 2 weeks. Alternatively, freeze it in portions for longer storage. Thaw and reheat before use.

Smoked Aioli

Ingredients:

2 large egg yolks
2 cloves garlic, minced
1 tablespoon (15ml) lemon juice
1 teaspoon (5ml) Dijon mustard
1 cup (240ml) olive oil
Salt and pepper to taste
Wood chips for smoking (hickory, applewood, etc.)

Smoking Process:

1. Soak wood chips in water for at least 30 minutes.

2. Preheat your BBQ smoker to 225°F (107°C) using indirect heat.

3. In a heatproof bowl or container suitable for smoking, combine the egg yolks, minced garlic, lemon juice, and Dijon mustard. Mix thoroughly.

4. Place the bowl or container on the smoker grates.

5. Smoke the mixture uncovered for about 15-20 minutes, using the soaked wood chips for smoke infusion.

6. Remove the smoked mixture from the smoker and let it cool to room temperature.

7. Once cooled, transfer the smoked mixture to a blender or food processor.

8. While blending, slowly drizzle in the olive oil until the aioli emulsifies and reaches a creamy consistency.

9. Season with salt and pepper to taste.

Resting:

- Allow the smoked aioli to rest and meld flavors for at least 30 minutes before serving.

Storage Recommendations:

- Store any leftover smoked aioli in an airtight container in the refrigerator for up to 3-4 days. Use it as a flavorful condiment or dip.

Smoked Chipotle Ketchup

Ingredients:

28 ounces (800g) canned crushed tomatoes
1/2 cup (120ml) apple cider vinegar
1/4 cup (60g) brown sugar
2 chipotle peppers in adobo sauce, chopped
1 tablespoon (15ml) adobo sauce (from the chipotle peppers can)
1 small onion, finely chopped
2 cloves garlic, minced
1 teaspoon (5ml) smoked paprika
1 teaspoon (5ml) ground mustard
1/2 teaspoon (2.5ml) ground cinnamon
1/2 teaspoon (2.5ml) salt
1/4 teaspoon (1.25ml) ground cloves

Smoking Process:

1. Preheat your BBQ smoker to 225°F (107°C) using indirect heat.

2. In a large, heatproof pan or skillet suitable for smoking, combine the crushed tomatoes, apple cider vinegar, brown sugar, chopped chipotle peppers, adobo

sauce, chopped onion, minced garlic, smoked paprika, ground mustard, ground cinnamon, salt, and ground cloves.

3. Place the pan on the smoker grates.

4. Smoke the mixture, uncovered, for about 2-3 hours, stirring occasionally to infuse the flavors and allow the sauce to thicken slightly.

5. Once the ketchup has reached the desired smoky flavor and consistency, remove it from the smoker.

Resting:

- Let the smoked chipotle ketchup cool to room temperature.

Storage Recommendations:

- Store the leftover smoked chipotle ketchup in a sealed jar or airtight container in the refrigerator for up to 2-3 weeks. Use it as a delicious condiment for various dishes, burgers, fries, and more.

Smoked Garlic Butter

Ingredients:

1 cup (227g) unsalted butter, softened
6 cloves garlic, minced
1 teaspoon (5ml) olive oil
Wood chips for smoking (hickory, applewood, etc.)

Smoking Process:

1. Preheat your BBQ smoker to 225°F (107°C) using indirect heat.
2. In a heatproof dish, combine the softened butter and minced garlic.
3. Drizzle the olive oil over the mixture and gently stir to incorporate.
4. Create a small pouch using aluminum foil to hold the butter mixture.
5. Place the pouch directly on the smoker grates.
6. Smoke the butter mixture for about 1 hour, ensuring it gets adequate smoke exposure.

7. Remove the pouch from the smoker.

Resting:

- Let the smoked garlic butter cool to room temperature.

Storage Recommendations:

- Store the smoked garlic butter in an airtight container in the refrigerator for up to 2 weeks or freeze it for longer-term storage. Use it as a flavorful spread for bread, seasoning for grilled dishes, or to enhance the taste of various recipes.

Smoked Jalapeño Hot Sauce

Ingredients:

1 pound (450g) fresh jalapeño peppers
6 cloves garlic, peeled
2 cups (480ml) white vinegar
1 cup (240ml) water
1 tablespoon (15ml) sugar
1 tablespoon (15ml) salt
Wood chips for smoking (hickory, mesquite, etc.)

Smoking Process:

1. Preheat your BBQ smoker to 225°F (107°C) using indirect heat.

2. Wash and dry the jalapeño peppers. Cut off the stems and slice them in half lengthwise. Remove the seeds and ribs for a milder sauce or leave some for extra heat.

3. Place the halved jalapeños and peeled garlic cloves on a smoker-safe tray or foil-lined tray.

4. Smoke the jalapeños and garlic in the smoker for about 1-2 hours, or until they develop a smoky flavor and the peppers are slightly softened.

5. Remove the smoked jalapeños and garlic from the smoker and let them cool.

Making the Hot Sauce:

1. In a blender or food processor, combine the smoked jalapeños, smoked garlic, white vinegar, water, sugar, and salt.

2. Blend until smooth and well combined.

3. Pour the mixture into a saucepan and bring it to a gentle simmer over medium heat.

4. Simmer for 10-15 minutes, stirring occasionally.

5. Let the hot sauce cool to room temperature.

Storage Recommendations:

- Transfer the smoked jalapeño hot sauce to sterilized bottles or jars. Store it in the refrigerator for up to 1 month. For longer-term storage, consider canning or freezing it in airtight containers. Adjust the spiciness by including more or fewer seeds and ribs from the jalapeños. Enjoy this flavorful sauce on various dishes or as a spicy condiment.

Smoked Pickles

Ingredients:

2 pounds (900g) pickling cucumbers, sliced
2 cups (480ml) white vinegar
2 cups (480ml) water
2 tablespoons (30g) pickling salt
2 tablespoons (25g) sugar
2 cloves garlic, peeled
1 teaspoon (5g) black peppercorns
1 teaspoon (5g) mustard seeds
Wood chips for smoking (applewood, cherry, etc.)

Smoking Process:

1. Preheat your BBQ smoker to 225°F (107°C) using indirect heat.

2. In a large heatproof dish or aluminum pan suitable for smoking, combine the white vinegar, water, pickling salt, sugar, garlic cloves, black peppercorns, and mustard seeds. Mix until the salt and sugar dissolve.

3. Add the sliced pickling cucumbers to the mixture in the pan.

4. Place the pan with the cucumbers and brine on the smoker grates.

5. Smoke the pickles in the smoker for about 1 hour, ensuring they absorb the smoky flavors.

6. Remove the pan from the smoker and let the smoked pickles cool to room temperature.

Resting:

- Once cooled, cover the smoked pickles with a lid or transfer them to airtight containers.

Storage Recommendations:

- Store the smoked pickles in the refrigerator for up to 2-3 weeks. Enjoy these uniquely smoky pickles as a zesty snack or as a complement to sandwiches, burgers, or salads.

Smoked Salsa

Ingredients:

2 pounds (900g) tomatoes, halved
1 large onion, peeled and quartered
2 jalapeño peppers, halved and seeded
3 cloves garlic, peeled
1 bell pepper, halved and seeded
1 tablespoon (15ml) olive oil
Juice of 1 lime
1 teaspoon (5g) salt
1 teaspoon (2g) smoked paprika
1 teaspoon (2g) ground cumin
Fresh cilantro, chopped (optional)
Wood chips for smoking (hickory, oak, etc.)

Smoking Process:

1. Preheat your BBQ smoker to 225°F (107°C) using indirect heat.

2. Place the halved tomatoes, quartered onion, halved jalapeños, garlic cloves, and halved bell pepper in a smoker-safe tray or on foil-lined trays.

3. Lightly drizzle olive oil over the vegetables and toss to coat evenly.

4. Place the tray with the vegetables in the smoker.

5. Smoke the vegetables for about 1-2 hours or until they have a slightly charred appearance and are softened.

6. Remove the smoked vegetables from the smoker and let them cool.

Making the Salsa:

1. Once cooled, chop the smoked tomatoes, onion, jalapeños, garlic, and bell pepper to your desired consistency and place them in a mixing bowl.

2. Add lime juice, salt, smoked paprika, and ground cumin. Mix well.

3. If desired, stir in chopped cilantro for added flavor.

4. Let the flavors meld together by allowing the salsa to rest in the refrigerator for at least an hour before serving.

Storage Recommendations:

- Store the smoked salsa in an airtight container in the refrigerator for up to 5-7 days. Enjoy this smoky salsa with tortilla chips, tacos, grilled meats, or as a flavorful topping.

Smoked Mustard Sauce

Ingredients:

1 cup (240g) yellow mustard
1/4 cup (60ml) apple cider vinegar
1/4 cup (60ml) honey
1/4 cup (60ml) maple syrup
2 tablespoons (30ml) Worcestershire sauce
1 tablespoon (15ml) hot sauce (adjust to taste)
1 teaspoon (5g) smoked paprika
1/2 teaspoon (2g) garlic powder
1/2 teaspoon (2g) onion powder
1/2 teaspoon (3g) salt
1/2 teaspoon (1g) black pepper
Wood chips for smoking (pecan, mesquite, etc.)

Smoking Process:

1. Preheat your BBQ smoker to 225°F (107°C) using indirect heat.

2. In a heatproof dish suitable for smoking, combine the yellow mustard, apple cider vinegar, honey, maple syrup, Worcestershire sauce, hot sauce, smoked

paprika, garlic powder, onion powder, salt, and black pepper. Mix until well combined.

3. Place the dish with the mustard sauce on the smoker grate.

4. Smoke the mustard sauce for about 1 hour, ensuring it absorbs the smoky flavors while occasionally stirring.

5. Remove the dish from the smoker and let the smoked mustard sauce cool to room temperature.

Resting:

- Once cooled, transfer the smoked mustard sauce to a clean, airtight container.

Storage Recommendations:

- Store the smoked mustard sauce in the refrigerator for up to 2-3 weeks. Use this flavorful sauce as a condiment for sandwiches, burgers, grilled meats, or as a dipping sauce.

Smoked Cranberry Sauce

Ingredients:

12 ounces (340g) fresh cranberries
1 cup (240ml) orange juice
3/4 cup (150g) granulated sugar
1 cinnamon stick
Zest of 1 orange
Pinch of salt
Wood chips for smoking (cherry, apple, etc.)

Smoking Process:

1. Preheat your BBQ smoker to 225°F (107°C) using indirect heat.

2. In a heatproof dish suitable for smoking, combine the fresh cranberries, orange juice, granulated sugar, cinnamon stick, orange zest, and a pinch of salt.

3. Place the dish with the cranberry mixture on the smoker grate.

4. Smoke the cranberry mixture for about 1 to 1.5 hours, ensuring it absorbs the smoky flavors. Stir occasionally to mix the flavors evenly.

5. Remove the dish from the smoker and let the smoked cranberry sauce cool to room temperature.

Resting:

- Once cooled, discard the cinnamon stick and transfer the smoked cranberry sauce to a clean, airtight container.

Storage Recommendations:

- Store the smoked cranberry sauce in the refrigerator for up to 1-2 weeks. It serves as a delightful accompaniment to poultry, sandwiches, or as a topping for desserts like cheesecake or ice cream.

Smoked Honey Glaze

Ingredients:

1 cup (240 ml) honey
1/4 cup (60 ml) water
1 teaspoon (5 ml) vanilla extract
Wood chips for smoking (apple, hickory, etc.)

Smoking Process:

1. Preheat your BBQ smoker to 225°F (107°C) using indirect heat.

2. In a heatproof dish suitable for smoking, combine the honey, water, and vanilla extract.

3. Place the dish with the honey mixture onto the smoker grate.

4. Smoke the honey mixture for about 1 hour, allowing it to absorb the smoky essence. Stir occasionally to ensure even smoking.

5. Remove the dish from the smoker and let the smoked honey glaze cool to room temperature.

Resting:

- Once cooled, transfer the smoked honey glaze to a clean, airtight jar or container.

Storage Recommendations:

- Store the smoked honey glaze at room temperature in a sealed container for up to a few weeks. If it crystallizes, gently warm it in a water bath or microwave to liquefy before using. Great for drizzling over desserts, adding to marinades, or glazing meats and vegetables.

BEVERAGES

Old Fashioned Cocktail

Ingredients:

2 oz (60 ml) bourbon
1 sugar cube or 1/2 oz (15 ml) simple syrup
2 dashes Angostura bitters
Orange peel
Ice cubes
Wood chips for smoking (cherry, oak, etc.)

Smoking Process:

1. Set up your BBQ smoker for cold smoking. Place the bourbon in a shallow, heatproof container suitable for smoking.

2. Light the smoker and add the wood chips according to the manufacturer's instructions for cold smoking.

3. Place the container with the bourbon inside the smoker, ensuring it remains cold. Let it smoke for about 30-45 minutes.

4. Remove the bourbon from the smoker and allow it to rest at room temperature for 10-15 minutes to mellow the smoky flavors.

Preparing the Cocktail:

1. In an Old Fashioned glass, muddle the sugar cube with bitters or use simple syrup.

2. Add ice cubes to the glass.

3. Pour the smoked bourbon over the ice.

4. Stir gently to combine the ingredients.

5. Express the oil from the orange peel over the drink by holding it over the glass, skin side down, and twisting to release the oils. Rub the peel around the rim before dropping it into the drink.

Storage Recommendations:

- This cocktail is best enjoyed fresh. If preparing smoked bourbon in advance, store it in a sealed bottle at room temperature until ready to use, ensuring it's consumed within a reasonable timeframe.

Apple Cider

Ingredients:

1 gallon (3.8 liters) apple cider
Wood chips (applewood, cherry, or hickory)

Smoking Process:

1. Pour the apple cider into a large, heatproof container suitable for smoking.

2. Set up your BBQ smoker for cold smoking.

3. Light the smoker and add the wood chips according to the manufacturer's instructions for cold smoking.

4. Place the container with the apple cider inside the smoker, ensuring it remains cold. Let it smoke for about 30-45 minutes.

5. Remove the container from the smoker and let the smoked cider rest at room temperature for 10-15 minutes to infuse the smoky flavors.

Storage Recommendations:

- Store any leftover smoked apple cider in a sealed container in the refrigerator. Consume within 3-4 days for the best flavor. Shake or stir well before serving if any settling occurs.

Lemonade

Ingredients:

8-10 lemons, halved
1 cup (200g) granulated sugar
6 cups (1.5 liters) water
Wood chips (fruitwood like apple or cherry works well)

Smoking Process:

1. Preheat your BBQ smoker for cold smoking.

2. Place the halved lemons, cut side up, on a tray suitable for smoking.

3. Add the wood chips to the smoker according to the manufacturer's instructions for cold smoking.

4. Put the tray of lemons in the smoker and smoke for about 20-25 minutes.

5. Remove the smoked lemons from the smoker and let them cool at room temperature for 5-10 minutes.

Lemonade Preparation:

1. While the smoked lemons cool, juice them into a pitcher. Discard any seeds.

2. In a saucepan, combine the sugar and water. Heat over medium heat until the sugar dissolves completely, creating a simple syrup. Let it cool.

3. Pour the simple syrup into the pitcher with the smoked lemon juice. Stir well to combine.

4. Refrigerate the smoked lemonade until thoroughly chilled.

Storage Recommendations:

- Store any leftover smoked lemonade in a sealed container in the refrigerator for up to 3-4 days. Stir or shake well before serving if any settling occurs.

Iced Tea

Ingredients:

6 cups (1.5 liters) water
6-8 tea bags (black tea or your preferred variety)
Wood chips suitable for smoking (fruitwood like apple or cherry works well)
Sweetener (sugar, honey, or simple syrup) (optional)
Lemon slices, fresh mint, or other garnishes (optional)

Smoking Process:

1. Preheat your BBQ smoker for cold smoking.

2. Pour the water into a heatproof container suitable for smoking.

3. Place the container of water in the smoker and smoke it for about 30-40 minutes using the wood chips, following the manufacturer's instructions for cold smoking.

4. Remove the smoked water from the smoker and let it cool to room temperature.

Tea Preparation:

1. In a large pitcher, steep the tea bags in the smoked water for about 5-10 minutes, or until desired strength is reached. Remove the tea bags.

2. Add sweetener if desired, stirring until dissolved.

3. Refrigerate the smoked iced tea until thoroughly chilled before serving

Storage Recommendations:

- Store any leftover smoked iced tea in a sealed container in the refrigerator for up to 2-3 days. Stir well before serving if any settling occurs.

Moscow Mule

Ingredients:

2 oz (60 ml) vodka
1 oz (30 ml) fresh lime juice
4-6 oz (120-180 ml) ginger beer
Ice cubes
Wood chips suitable for smoking (applewood, cherrywood, or hickory)
Lime wedges and mint leaves for garnish

Smoking Process:

1. Preheat your BBQ smoker for cold smoking.

2. Fill a heatproof container with the vodka and place it in the smoker.

3. Smoke the vodka for about 30-40 minutes using the wood chips, following the manufacturer's instructions for cold smoking.

4. Remove the smoked vodka from the smoker and allow it to cool to room temperature.

Drink Preparation:

1. Fill a copper mug (or a glass of choice) with ice cubes.

2. Pour the smoked vodka and fresh lime juice over the ice.

3. Top off with ginger beer and gently stir.

4. Garnish with lime wedges and mint leaves.

Storage Recommendations:

- There won't typically be leftovers from a prepared cocktail, but if there are, store the cocktail components separately (smoked vodka in a sealed bottle, lime juice in a container) in the refrigerator for up to a week. Reassemble and remix when ready to enjoy.

Cranberry Punch

Ingredients:

4 cups (950 ml) cranberry juice
2 cups (475 ml) apple juice
1 cup (240 ml) orange juice
1/4 cup (60 ml) lemon juice
1/4 cup (60 ml) maple syrup or honey
1 cinnamon stick
4-5 whole cloves
1 cup (240 ml) fresh cranberries
Ice cubes
Wood chips suitable for smoking (applewood, cherrywood, or hickory)

Smoking Process:

1. Preheat your BBQ smoker for cold smoking.

2. Pour the cranberry juice, apple juice, orange juice, lemon juice, and maple syrup (or honey) into a heatproof container.

3. Add the cinnamon stick, cloves, and fresh cranberries into the container with the juice mixture.

4. Place the container in the smoker and cold smoke for about 30-40 minutes, using the wood chips according to the smoker's instructions.

5. Remove the smoked juice mixture from the smoker and let it cool to room temperature.

Drink Preparation:

1. Strain the smoked juice mixture into a punch bowl or pitcher, discarding the cloves, cinnamon stick, and any remnants.

2. Add ice cubes to the punch bowl or pitcher.

3. Stir well before serving.

Storage Recommendations:

- Store any leftover smoked punch in an airtight container in the refrigerator for up to 2-3 days. Give it a good stir before serving again.

Smoked Hot Chocolate

Ingredients:

4 cups (950 ml) milk
1/2 cup (120 ml) heavy cream
8 ounces (230g) dark chocolate, chopped
1/4 cup (50g) granulated sugar
1 teaspoon vanilla extract
Pinch of salt
Marshmallows (for serving)
Wood chips suitable for smoking (hickory, cherrywood, or oak)

Smoking Process:

1. Preheat your BBQ smoker for cold smoking.

2. In a heatproof dish or tray, spread out the chopped dark chocolate.

3. Place the dish with the chocolate in the smoker and cold smoke for about 30-40 minutes, using the wood chips according to the smoker's instructions.

4. Remove the smoked chocolate from the smoker and let it cool slightly.

Drink Preparation:

1. In a saucepan over medium-low heat, combine the milk, heavy cream, sugar, vanilla extract, and a pinch of salt.

2. Warm the mixture gently until it's hot but not boiling, stirring occasionally.

3. Add the smoked chocolate to the warm milk mixture and whisk until the chocolate is completely melted and the mixture is smooth and creamy.

Resting:

- Let the smoked hot chocolate rest for a couple of minutes before serving to allow the flavors to meld.

Serve:

- Ladle the smoked hot chocolate into mugs and top with marshmallows or whipped cream if desired.

Storage Recommendations:

- Store any leftover smoked hot chocolate in an airtight container in the refrigerator for up to 2 days. Reheat gently on the stovetop or in the microwave before serving again.

Smoked Coffee

Ingredients:

4 cups (950 ml) water
1/2 cup (60g) coarsely ground coffee beans
Wood chips suitable for smoking (applewood, mesquite, or pecan)

Smoking Process:

1. Preheat your BBQ smoker for cold smoking.

2. Spread the coarsely ground coffee beans in a thin, even layer on a baking sheet or in a shallow heatproof dish.

3. Place the dish or baking sheet of coffee grounds in the smoker and cold smoke for about 1-2 hours, using the wood chips according to the smoker's instructions.

4. Remove the smoked coffee grounds from the smoker and let them cool completely.

Drink Preparation:

1. Heat the water in a pot or kettle until it reaches just below boiling.
2. Place the smoked coffee grounds in a heatproof container or French press.
3. Slowly pour the hot water over the smoked coffee grounds, ensuring they are fully immersed in the water.
4. Let the coffee steep for about 4-5 minutes, depending on desired strength.
5. Slowly press down the plunger if using a French press or strain the coffee through a fine-mesh sieve or coffee filter to separate the grounds from the brewed coffee.

Resting:

- Let the smoked coffee rest for a couple of minutes before serving to allow the flavors to settle.

Serve:

- Pour the smoked coffee into your desired vessel and enjoy as desired, with milk, cream, sugar, or as black coffee.

Storage Recommendations:

- Smoked coffee can be stored in an airtight container at room temperature for up to a week. Keep it away from moisture and direct sunlight to maintain freshness.

Smoked Eggnog

Ingredients:

6 large eggs
3/4 cup (150g) granulated sugar
2 cups (475ml) whole milk
1 cup (240ml) heavy cream
1 teaspoon (5ml) vanilla extract
1/2 teaspoon (2.5ml) ground cinnamon
1/2 teaspoon (2.5ml) ground nutmeg
Pinch of salt
Wood chips suitable for smoking (such as hickory, applewood, or cherry)

Smoking Process:

1. In a heatproof dish or shallow pan, carefully place the eggs (in their shells) and set aside.

2. Preheat your BBQ smoker for cold smoking.

3. Add the wood chips to the smoker according to the manufacturer's instructions.

4. Place the dish of eggs in the smoker and cold smoke them for about 30-40 minutes.

5. Remove the smoked eggs from the smoker and set them aside to cool.

Eggnog Preparation:

1. Once the smoked eggs have cooled, crack them open and separate the yolks from the whites. Discard the whites or save them for another use.

2. In a mixing bowl, whisk the egg yolks and sugar together until creamy and slightly thickened.

3. In a saucepan over medium heat, combine the milk, heavy cream, vanilla extract, cinnamon, nutmeg, and salt. Heat the mixture until it's just about to simmer, stirring occasionally.

4. Gradually pour the hot milk mixture into the egg yolk mixture, whisking constantly to prevent the eggs from curdling.

5. Return the combined mixture to the saucepan and continue cooking over low heat, stirring continuously, until the eggnog thickens slightly. Do not let it boil.

6. Once thickened to your desired consistency, remove the eggnog from the heat and let it cool to room temperature.

7. Chill the smoked eggnog in the refrigerator for at least 2-3 hours or until thoroughly chilled.

Resting:

- Allow the flavors to meld by letting the eggnog rest in the refrigerator for a few hours or overnight.

Serve:

- Before serving, stir or whisk the eggnog to recombine any separated ingredients. Optionally, garnish with a sprinkle of ground nutmeg or a cinnamon stick.

Storage Recommendations:

- Smoked eggnog can be stored in a sealed container in the refrigerator for up to 3-4 days. Shake or stir well before serving leftovers.

Smoked Sangria

Ingredients:

1 bottle (750ml) red wine
1/4 cup (60ml) brandy
2 cups (475ml) orange juice
1 cup (240ml) cranberry juice
1 orange, sliced
1 lemon, sliced
1 lime, sliced
1 apple, cored and sliced
1/2 cup (100g) mixed berries (such as strawberries, raspberries, blueberries)
2 cinnamon sticks
1/4 cup (60g) granulated sugar (adjust to taste)
Ice cubes
Wood chips suitable for smoking (e.g., applewood, cherry, or oak)

Smoking Process:

1. In a large heatproof container or shallow pan, combine the sliced fruits, berries, cinnamon sticks, and sugar. Mix well.

2. Preheat your BBQ smoker for cold smoking.
3. Add the wood chips to the smoker according to the manufacturer's instructions.
4. Place the container with the fruit mixture in the smoker and cold smoke for about 30-40 minutes, infusing the fruits with smoky flavor. Ensure the container is covered to prevent ash or debris from falling into the sangria ingredients.
5. Remove the smoked fruit mixture from the smoker and set it aside.

Sangria Preparation:

1. In a large pitcher or bowl, combine the red wine, brandy, orange juice, and cranberry juice.
2. Add the smoked fruit mixture, including any juices released during the smoking process, into the pitcher with the liquid ingredients.
3. Stir the sangria well to combine all the flavors.
4. Refrigerate the sangria to let the flavors meld for at least 2-3 hours or overnight.

Resting:

- Allow the sangria to rest in the refrigerator to intensify the smoky flavor.

Serve:

- When ready to serve, fill glasses with ice cubes and pour the smoked sangria over the ice.
- Garnish each glass with a slice of smoked fruit from the pitcher if desired.

Storage Recommendations:

- Store any leftover smoked sangria in a sealed container in the refrigerator for up to 2-3 days. The flavors may continue to meld, enhancing the taste over time. Stir or shake well before serving leftovers.

A SPECIAL THANK YOU

To all our cherished friends who have become part of the Saucy Pig family through your unwavering support, this book's pages hold not just recipes, but the essence of our shared joy and love for good food and company.

As this book concludes, we extend our heartfelt gratitude to each of you who has embraced our culinary journey. Your enthusiasm, encouragement, and warmth have made our table richer, our recipes more vibrant, and our celebrations brighter.

May this holiday season be adorned with the laughter of loved ones, the aroma of delightful dishes, and the joy of shared moments. From our Saucy Pig family to yours, we wish you a Merry Christmas filled with warmth, love, and delicious feasts. As we bid adieu to this year, may the upcoming New Year bring you prosperity, joy, and endless culinary adventures.

Thank you again for being part of our story.

Merry Christmas and a Prosperous New Year!

Cheers to many more delightful moments shared around the table!

The Saucy Pig

www.thesaucypig.es

thesaucypig@hotmail.com